# Quotations for Martial Artists

# Quotations for Martial Artists

◆

## Hundreds of Inspirational Quotes to Motivate and Enlighten the Modern Warrior

*Compiled by John David Moore*

Writers Club Press
New York Lincoln Shanghai

# Quotations for Martial Artists
## Hundreds of Inspirational Quotes to Motivate and Enlighten the Modern Warrior

Writers Club Press
an imprint of iUniverse, Inc.

For information address:
iUniverse, Inc.
2021 Pine Lake Road, Suite 100
Lincoln, NE 68512
www.iuniverse.com

For more information about professional martial arts training products and services please see author's web site at www.martialtrainingsystems.com

ISBN: 0-595-26492-1

Printed in the United States of America

*To Myra, my inspiration and motivation.*
*To Sensei Peter Freedman, my teacher. You taught me that martial arts can be quirky, funny, deadly, spiritual, and loving.*

# Contents

# Introduction

Many years ago, when I began my study of Ketsugo Jujutsu under the tutelage of Sensei Peter Freedman I began to collect quotes. I love quotes and use them frequently when I am writing—even in simple emails to friends. The right quote can capture an essential meaning and, if it's from a strong source, provide credibility.

This is a collection of quotes specifically compiled for martial artists. Most of the quotes are not from martial arts sources, but many are. You will find quotes here from politicians, coaches, samurai, teachers, writers, poets and more. These quotes have been chosen and organized to be useful for martial artists. They certainly can be used for one's own personal inspiration. I have also had teachers who would read a choice quote or passage from a book before or during a class to elucidate a lesson.

I have divided this collection into thirteen categories. These categories are my own, and I have attempted to provide categories that would be useful to the martial artist. Certainly there are quotes in this book that would fit equally well into any number of categories. I have placed the quotes where I feel they best belong in the order that I feel they belong. If, for example, you turn to the section on teaching; you will find quotes related to teaching.

You will notice that there is a section on humor here. For many studying in a "traditional" martial arts environment—humor may seem out of place. That's too bad. Humor is part of the human experience and the ability to enjoy oneself while taking one's martial arts development seriously is certainly a spiritual skill. Humor creates a positive emotional environment, and pedagogical and neurological studies have proven that people learn better when they are having fun.

There may be quotes included in this book that may seem questionable or objectionable. If you are offended by anything in here…you're welcome. Seriously. I believe that it is a spiritually empowering lessons of the martial arts to be able to analyze and recognize why things make us feel the way we do. If you are offended by somebody's words, do not dismiss them, and do not dishonor your feelings, but ask yourself why you feel this way. Everything is a matter of perspective and feeling angry or offended can be an opportunity for development—it's up to you. This simple exercise has had profound effects on my own self-discovery and I encourage you to try it whenever you feel "negative" emotions.

Lastly, there are literally hundreds of quotes here gathered from hundreds of sources. It has been my intention to represent and attribute these quotes as accurately as possible. I am human and there may be errors in this book. I apologize in advance for any misquotations or misattributions in this book. If you find any errors here, and are the first one to report them to me via my web site (**www. martialtrainingsystems.com**), I will send you a free t-shirt and a promise to correct the error in future editions of this book

# 1

## *Focus*

SHUCHU RYOKU—Focus all your energy to one point.

—Shioda, Gozo


At the instant a warrior confronts a foe, all things come into focus.

—Ueshiba, Morihei


Power is not revealed by striking hard or often, but by striking true.

—Honore de Balzac


I know that I'm never as good or bad as any single performance. I've never believed my critics or my worshippers, and I've always been able to leave the game at the arena.

—Charles Barkley

There are only two options regarding commitment. You're either IN or you're OUT. There's no such thing as life in-between.

—Pat Riley

When you're riding, only the race in which you're riding is important.

—Bill Shoemaker

I learned that if you want to make it bad enough, no matter how bad it is, you can make it.

—Gale Sayers

Setting a goal is not the main thing. It is deciding how you will go about achieving it and staying with that plan.

—Tom Landry

Show me a guy who's afraid to look bad, and I'll show you a guy you can beat every time.

—Lou Brock

My thoughts before a big race are usually pretty simple. I tell myself: "Get out of the blocks, run your race, stay relaxed. If you run your race, you'll win…. Channel your energy. Focus."

—Carl Lewis

He who hesitates, meditates in a horizontal position

—Ed Parker

Start living now. Stop saving the good china for that special occasion. Stop withholding your love until that special person materializes. Every day you are alive is a special occasion. Every minute, every breath, is a gift from God.

—Mary Manin Morrissey

Sword and mind must be united. Technique by itself is insufficient, and spirit alone is not enough.

—Yamada Jirokichi

The time to strike is when the opportunity presents itself.

—6th Code of Isshinryu Karatedo

If you chase two rabbits, both will escape.

—Anonymous

Only one-in-a-million will strive with full intent and courage to become the unique somebody that person was created and destined to be! And yet each of us was destined at birth to be a one-in-a-million person!

—Dr. William Mitchell

Set your goals high, and don't stop till you get there.

—Bo Jackson

Wherever you go, go with all your heart.

—Confucius

Each of us has a fire in our hearts for something. It's our goal in life to find it and keep it lit.

—Mary Lou Retton

Try not! Do, or do not. There is no try.

—Yoda

The fighter is to be always single-minded with one object in view: to fight, looking neither backward nor sidewise. To go straight forward in order to crush the enemy is all that is necessary for him.

—Daisetz Suzuki

The focused mind can pierce through stone.

—Japanese maxim

Patience is also a form of action.

—Auguste Rodin

Your work is to discover your work and then with all your heart to give yourself to it.

—Buddha

In extreme situations, the entire universe becomes our foe; at such critical times, unity of mind and technique is essential—do not let your heart waver!

—Ueshiba, Morihei

The warrior's intention should be simply to grasp his sword and to die.

—Kiyomasa Kato

Under pressure you can perform fifteen percent better or worse.

—Scott Hamilton

In the moment of action remember the value of silence and order.

—Phormio of Athens

Fiddling with this and that technique is of no avail. Simply act decisively without reserve!

—Ueshiba, Morihei

Ain't no chance if you don't take it.

—Guy Clark

# 2

## *Teaching*

You cannot teach a man anything. You can only help him discover it within himself.

—Galileo

The teacher, if indeed wise, does not bid you to enter the house of their wisdom, but leads you to the threshold of your own mind.

—Kahil Gibran

The teaching of one virtuous person can influence many; that which has been learned well by one generation can be passed on to a hundred.

—Kano, Jigoro

Where questioning is rewarded, virtues are promoted, respect is demanded, and love is central.

—L'abri

Experience is a good teacher, but she sends in terrific bills.

—Minna Antrim

Pain is the best instructor, but no one wants to go to his class.

—Choi, Hong Hi

Teaching is more difficult than learning because what teaching calls for is this: to let learn. The real teacher, in fact, let nothing else be learned than learning. His conduct, therefore, often produces the impression that we properly learn nothing from him, if by "learning" we now suddenly understand merely the procurement of useful information.

—Martin Heidegger

To teach is to learn twice.

—Joseph Joubert

To lead an untrained people to war is to throw them away.

—Confucius

I don't look for anything when I train someone…their best qualities come to me…they (qualities) show themselves…It's the way you teach that should be addressed…when an individual listens with 'confidence' rather than through 'intimidation', you would be amazed at what comes up to the surface.

—Glen Doyle


True teaching, then, is not that which gives knowledge, but that which stimulates pupils to gain it.

—Milton Gregory


Teachers open the door. You enter by yourself.

—Chinese proverb


A teacher affects eternity; he can never tell where his influence stops.

—Henry Adams


Good teaching is one-fourth preparation and three-fourths theater.

—Gail Godwin

The whole art of teaching is only the art of awakening the natural curiosity of young minds for the purpose of satisfying it afterwards.

—Anatole France

You're aware the boy failed my grade school math class, I take it? And not that many years later he's teaching college. Now I ask you: Is that the sorriest indictment of the American educational system you ever heard? No aptitude at all for long division, but never mind. It's him they ask to split the atom. How he talked his way into the Nobel Prize is beyond me. But then, I suppose it's like the man says, "It's not what you know…"

—Karl Arbeiter speaking about Albert Einstein

The true teacher defends his pupils against his own personal influence.

—Amos Bronson Alcott

Thoroughly to teach another is the best way to learn for yourself.

—Tyron Edwards

The strongest human instinct is to impart information, the second strongest is to resist it.

—Kenneth Graham

I imagine good teaching as a circle of earnest people sitting down to
each other meaningful questions. I don't see it as the handing down of
answers. So much of what passes for teaching is merely a pointing out
of what items to want.

—Alice Walker

# 3

## *Character*

The ultimate aim of karate lies not in victory or defeat but in the perfection of the character of its participants.

—Funakoshi, Gichin


Regret is an appalling waste of energy, you can't build on it; it's only good for wallowing in.

—Katherine Mansfield, Author


It's not just self defense, it's about…self control, body discipline, and mind discipline…and breath techniques. It involves yoga. It involves meditation. It's an art, not a sport.

—Elvis Presley.


The only place where success comes before work is in the dictionary.

—Vidal Sassoon

There are only two powers in the world…the sword and the spirit the long run, the sword is always defeated by the spirit.

—Napoleon Bonaparte

Never confuse someone else's inability to do something with its inability to be done.

—Steve Maraboli

He turned his own weapons upon himself, doing battle with his negative emotions.

—H.H. The Dalai Lama, speaking about Shantideva

I'm a great believer in luck, and I find the harder I work, the more I have of it.

—Thomas Jefferson

The path of the Warrior is lifelong, and mastery is often simply staying on the path.

—Richard Strozzi Heckler

...nced excellence, you will never again be content

The principle is competing against yourself. It's about self-improvement, about being better than you were the day before.

—Steve Young

It is not the accumulation of extraneous knowledge, but the realization of the self within, that constitutes true progress.

—Okakura Kakuzo

Only those who dare to fail greatly can ever achieve greatly.

—Robert F. Kennedy

Adversity causes some men to break; others to break records.

—William A. Ward

When you're playing against a stacked deck, compete even harder. Show the world how much you'll fight for the winner's circle. If you do, someday the cellophane will crackle off a fresh pack, one that belongs to you, and the cards will be stacked in your favor.

—Pat Riley

Ingenuity, plus courage, plus work, equals miracles.

—Bob Richards

Knowledge does not grow like a tree where you dig a hole, plant your feet, cover them with dirt, and pour water on them daily. Knowledge grows with time, work, and dedicated effort. It cannot come by any other means.

—Ed Parker.

The price of success is hard work, dedication to the job at hand, and the determination that whether we win or lose, we have applied the best of ourselves to the task at hand.

—Vince Lombardi

Mediocre people are always at their best.

—Colin Powell

The Way of a Warrior is based on humanity, love, and sincerity; the heart of martial valor is true bravery, wisdom, love, and friendship. Emphasis on the physical aspects of warriorship is futile, for the power of the body is always limited.

—Ueshiba, Morihei

When you were born, you cried and the world rejoiced. Live your life so that when you die, the world cries and you rejoice.

—Cherokee Expression

Have patience with all things, but chiefly have patience with yourself. Do not lose courage in considering you own imperfections but instantly set about remedying them—every day begin the task anew.

—Saint Francis de Sales

Talent develops in tranquility, character in the full current of human life.

—Johann Wolfgang von Goethe

The man who would be a warrior considers it his most basic intention to keep death always in mind, day and night, from the time he first picks up his chopsticks in celebrating his morning meal on New Year's Day to the evening of the last day of the year. When one constantly keeps death in mind, both loyalty and filial piety are realized, myriad evils and disasters are avoided, one is without illness and mishap, and lives out a long life. In addition, even his character is improved. Such are the many benifits of this act.

—Daidoji Yuzan

The price of success is hard work, dedication to the job at hand, and the determination that whether we win or lose, we have applied the best of ourselves to the task at hand.

—Vince Lombardi

The best way to judge a man's character is to see what he does when he thinks no one's looking.

—Jim Poserina

Every man has three characters—that which he exhibits, that which has, and that which he thinks he has.

—Alphonse Karr

For us, warriors are not what you think of as warriors. The warrior is not someone who fights, because no one has the right to take another's life. The warrior, for us, is one who sacrifices himself for the good of others. His task is to take care of the elderly, the defenseless, those who cannot provide for themselves, and above all, the children, the future of humanity.

—Sitting Bull

Excellence can be the only excepted outcome. Everything else is just warm up

—Ray Salomone


You have no control over what the other guy does. You only have control over what you do.

—A J Kitt


1. Do not think dishonestly.

2. The Way is in training.

3. Become acquainted with every art.

4. Know the Ways of all professions.

5. Distinguish between gain and loss in worldly matters.

6. Develop intuitive judgment and understanding for everything

7. Percieve those things which cannot be seen.

8. Pay attention even to trifles.

9. Do nothing which is of no use.

—Miyamoto, Musashi, A Book Of Five Rings (Go Rin No Sho)


The only way to have a friend is to be one.

—Ralph Waldo Emerson

You will become as small as your controlling desire; as great as your dominant aspiration.

—James Allen, Author

Loyalty and devotion lead to bravery. Bravery leads to the spirit of self-sacrifice. The spirit of self-sacrifice creates trust in the power of love.

—Ueshiba, Morihei

Each of us is an impregnable fortress that can be laid waste only from within.

—Timothy J. Flynn

Foster and polish the warrior spirit while serving in the world; illuminate the path according to your inner light.

—Ueshiba, Morihei

First see to it that you, yourself, are all right, then think of defeating an opponent.

—The Way of the Spear

I must respect the opinions of others even if I disgree with them.

—Herbert Lehman

The man who lives by himself and for himself is apt to be corrupted by the company he keeps.

—Charles Henry Parkhurst

Discipline strengthens the mind so that it becomes impervious to the corroding influence of fear.

—Bernard Montgomery

Class is an aura of confidence that is being sure without being cocky. Class has nothing to do with money. Class never runs scared. It is self-discipline and self-knowledge. It's the sure footedness that comes with having proved you can meet life.

—Ann Landers

The final aim of Judo, therefore, is to inculcate in the mind of man a spirit of respect for the principle of maximum efficiency and of mutual welfare and benefit, leading him so to practice them that man individually and collectively can attain to the highest state, and, at the same time, develop the body and learn the art of attack and defense.

—Kano, Jigoro

In War: Resolution In Defeat: Defiance In Victory: Magnanimity In Peace: Good Will

—Winston Churchill

Be grateful even for hardship, setbacks, and bad people. Dealing with such obstacles is an essential part of training in Aikido.

—Ueshiba, Morihei

Commitment in the face of conflict produces character.

—Anonymous

Your life is the sum result of all the choices you make, both consciously and unconsciously. If you can control the process of choosing, you can take control of all aspects of your life. You can find the freedom that comes from being in charge of yourself.

—Robert F. Bennett

I firmly believe that the only disability in life is a bad attitude.

—Scott Hamilton

Values are like fingerprints. Nobody's are the same, but you leave 'em all over everything you do.

—Elvis Presley

There's a big difference between confidence and conceit. To me, conceit is bragging about yourself. Being confident means you believe you can get the job done, but you know you can't get your job done unless you also have the confidence that the other guys are going to get their jobs done too. Without them, I'm nothing.

—Johnny Unitas

# 4

## *Defense*

This is the law:

There is no possible victory in defense, The Sword is more important than the shield, And skill is more important than either, The final weapon is the brain. All else is supplemental.

—John Steinbeck


Never give a sword to a man who can't dance

—Celtic Proverb


Even when called out by a single foe, remain on guard, for you are always surrounded by a host of enemies.

—Ueshiba, Morihei


I have a high art; I hurt with cruelty those who would damage me.

—Archilocus

When in doubt, knock 'em out

—"Big" Vinny Girolamo


An unwillingness to deal forcibly with violence does not equate to moral rectitude.

—Mary Malmros


When in trouble or in doubt, Cut down all who move about.

—Frederick J. Lovret


Even though surrounded by several enemies set to attack, fight with the thought that they are but one.

—Ueshiba, Morihei


Karate is a defensive art from beginning to end

—Funakoshi, Gichin


A warrior may choose pacifism. Others are condemned to it.

—Anonymous

When pure knuckles meet pure flesh, that's pure Karate, no matter who executes it or whatever style is involved.

—Ed Parker

When two tigers fight, one is certain to be maimed, and one to die.

—Master Funakoshi

Opponents confront us continually, but actually there is no opponent there. Enter deeply into an attack and neutralize it as you draw that misdirected force into your own sphere.

—Ueshiba, Morihei

Never do an enemy a small injury.

—Machiavelli

The right to defend oneself and one's loved ones from death and bodily injury at the hands of another should be paramount and inalienable.

—John David Moore

Don't hit at all if it can be avoided, but never hit softly.

—Theodore Roosevelt

If the enemy stays spirited it is difficult to crush him.

—Musashi, Miyamoto

If your opponent tries to pull you, let him pull. Don't pull against him; pull in unison with him.

—Ueshiba, Morihei

When, in a split second, your life is threatened, do you say, "Let me make sure my hand is on my hip, and my style is 'the' style?" When your life is in danger, do you argue about the method you will adhere to while saving yourself?, Why the duality?

—Bruce Lee

Let him smash your flesh, and you fracture his bone. Let him fracture your bone, and you take his life. Lay your life before him.

—Bruce Lee

When you have to kill a man, it costs nothing to be polite.

—Winston Churchill

Unarmed hand-to-hand fighting does not change through the a~~ge~~
only the name changes, and it has only one rule: do it first, do it fast,
do it dirtiest.

—Robert A. Heinlein

# 5

## *Victory*

Victory goes to the one who has no thought of himself

—Shinkage School of Swordsmanship

Success—my nomination for the single most important ingredient is energy well directed.

—Louis Lundborg

The minute you start talking about what you're going to do if you lose, you have lost.

—George Shultz

Winning is not a sometime thing; it's an all time thing. You don't win once in a while, you don't do things right once in a while, you do them right all the time. Winning is habit. Unfortunately, so is losing.

—Vince Lombardi

To succeed…You need to find something to hold on to, something to motivate you, something to inspire you.

—Tony Dorsett

Victories that are easy are cheap. Those only are worth having which come as the result of hard fighting.

—Henry Ward Beecher

You ask, What is our policy? I will say; "It is to wage war, by sea, land and air, with all our might and with all the strength that God can give us: to wage war against a monstrous tyranny, never surpassed in the dark lamentable catalogue of human crime. That is our policy." You ask, What is our aim? I can answer with one word: Victory—victory at all costs, victory in spite of all terror, victory however long and hard the road may be; for without victory there is no survival.

—Winston Churchill

War is a series of catastrophes that results in a victory.

—Georges Clemenceau

Be ashamed to die unless you have won some victory for humanity.

—Horace Mann

Before you can win a game, you have to not lose it.

—Chuck Noll


Never leave an enemy standing.

—Shaka Zulu


To win one hundred victories in one hundred battles is not the highest skill. To subdue the enemy without fighting is the highest skill.

—Sun-Tsu


Far better it is to dare mighty things, to win glorious triumphs even though checkered by failure, than to rank with those poor spirits who neither enjoy nor suffer much because they live in the gray twilight that knows neither victory nor defeat.

—Theodore Roosevelt


A winner never whines.

—Paul Brown

If you set a goal for yourself and are able to achieve it, you have won your race. Your goal can be to come in first, to improve your performance, or just finish the race—it's up to you.

—Dave Scott

When you are playing for the national championship, it's not a matter of life or death. It's more important than that.

—Duffy Daugherty

Most games are lost, not won.

—Casey Stengel

Winners never quit and quitters never win.

—Anonymous

You can prevent your opponent from defeating you through defense, but you cannot defeat him without taking the offensive.

—Sun Tzu

Looking to thine own duty thou shouldst not tremble; for there is nothing more welcome to a Kshattriya (Warrior) than righteous war offered unsought as an open door to heaven.

—The Bhagavad Gita


Victory goes to the player who makes the next-to-last mistake.

—Savielly Grigorievitch Tartakower


Opportunities multiply as they are seized.

—Sun Tzu


In war there is no substitute for victory.

—Douglas MacArthur


Victory is a political fiction.

—Anonymous

# 6

# *Courage*

Let's Roll

—Todd Beamer

One finds life through conquering the fear of death within one's mind. Empty the mind of all forms of attachment, make a go-for-broke charge and conquer the opponent with one decisive slash.

—Togo Shigekata.

To practice Zen or the Martial Arts, you must live intensely, whole-heartedly, without reserve—as if you might die in the next instant

—Taisen Deshimaru

Bravery is the capacity to perform properly even when scared half to death.

—Omar Bradley

It is not the critic who counts; not the man who points out how the strong man stumbles, or where the doer of deeds could have done them better. The credit belongs to the man who is actually in the arena, whose face is marred by dust and sweat and blood, who strives valiantly; who errs and comes short again and again; because there is not effort without error and shortcomings; but who does actually strive to do the deed; who knows the great enthusiasm, the great devotion, who spends himself in a worthy cause, who at the best knows in the end the triumph of high achievement and who at the worst, if he fails, at least he fails while daring greatly. So that his place shall never be with those cold and timid souls who know neither victory nor defeat.

—Theodore Roosevelt


The frightening nature of knowledge leaves one no alternative but to become a warrior.

—don Juan via Carlos Castenada


Courage is resistance to fear, mastery of fear, not absence of fear.

—Mark Twain


The first and great commandment is, Don't let them scare you.

—Elmer Davis

You learn you can do your best even when it's hard, even when you're tired and maybe hurting a little bit. It feels good to show some courage.

—Joe Namath

Courage is the price that life exacts for granting peace.

—Amelia Earhart

There's no substitute for guts.

—Paul "Bear" Bryant

It's lack of faith that makes people afraid of meeting challenges, and I believed in myself.

—Muhammad Ali

Of all hazards, fear is the worst.

—Sam Snead

Courage is contagious. When a brave man takes a stand, the spines of others are stiffened.

—Brian G. Jett

You need to play with supreme confidence, or else you'll lose again, and then losing becomes a habit.

—Joe Paterno

Courage is the art of being the only one who knows you're scared to death.

—Harold Wilson

Besides pride, loyalty, discipline, heart, and mind, confidence is the key to all the locks.

—Joe Paterno

Courage and perseverance have a magical talisman, before which difficulties disappear and obstacles vanish into air.

—John Quincy Adams

There is no greater solitude than the Samurai's, unless perhaps it be that of the tiger in the jungle

—Book of Bushido

Courage is the ladder on which all the other virtues mount.

—Claire Booth Luce

A timid person is frightened before a danger, a coward during the time, and a courageous person afterward.

—Jean Paul Richter

Courage is doing what you're afraid to do. There can be no courage unless you're scared.

—Eddie Rickenbacker

Courage is being scared to death but saddling up anyway.

—John Wayne

The only way to find the limits of the possible is by going beyond them to the impossible.

—Arthur C. Clarke

Indeed, no form of athletic endeavor can do more toward the restoration of confidence than successful participation in combative sport.

—Henry A. Stone

Life shrinks or expands in proportion to one's courage.

—Anais Nin

A ship in the harbor is safe. But that's not what ships are built for.

—Anonymous

You can become a winner only if you are willing to walk over the edge.

—Damon Runyon

Often the attack is not from an opponent, but from within, from our fears and doubts. Our ability to handle this sort of 'self-mugging', where we rob ourselves of time and energy and opportunity is far more impacting than an isolated physical attack. All lives are filled with confrontations…how we handle those confrontations, determines the quality of our day and ultimately the quality of our lives.

—Tony Blauer

Fear is the true opiate of combat.

—Anonymous

The end of our Way of the sword is to be fearless when confronting our inner enemies and our outer enemies.

—Tesshu Yamaoka

Whenever you meet difficult situations, dash forward bravely and joyfully.

—Tsunetomo Yamamoto

You may have to fight when there is no hope of victory, because it is better to perish than live as slaves.

—Sir Winston Churchill

Free of weakness, no-mindedly ignore the sharp attacks of your enemies: Step in and act!

—Ueshiba, Morihei

Do not look upon this world with fear and loathing. Bravely face whatever the gods offer.

—Ueshiba, Morihei

Take arrows in your forehead, but never in your back.

—Samurai maxim

I have accepted fear as part of life—specifically the fear of change. I have gone ahead despite the pounding in the heart that says turn back.

—Erica Jong

Go to the battlefield firmly confident of victory and you will come home with no wounds whatsoever.

—Kenshin Uesugi

A warrior must only take care that his spirit is never broken.

—Shissai

He who has a why to live for can bear almost any how.

—Friedrich Nietzsche

The Spartans do not enquire how many the enemy are, but where they are.

—Agis II

Courage, above all things, is the first quality of a warrior.

—Karl Von Clausewitz

Faced with what is right, to leave it undone shows a lack of courage.

—Confucius

The ordinary man is involved in action, the hero acts. An immense difference.

—Henry Miller


It is better to die on your feet than to live on your knees.

—Emiliano Zapata


You will never do anything in this world without courage. It is the greatest quality of the mind next to honor.

—James Allen


It is a brave act of valor to condemn death, but where life is more terrible than death it is then the truest valor to dare to live.

—Sir Thomas Brown


They've got us surrounded again, the poor bastards.

—Creighton W. Abrams


It's not the size of the dog in the fight, it's the size of the fight in the dog.

—Mark Twain

# 7

## *Leadership*

Do not follow where the path may lead. Go instead where there is no path and leave a trail.

—Anonymous

If you are not making anyone mad, you are not getting anything done.

—Paul McNicol

We must either find a way or make one.

—Hannibal

The leaders I met, whatever walk of life they were from, whatever institutions they were presiding over, always referred back to the same failure something that happened to them that was personally difficult, even traumatic, something that made them feel that desperate sense of hitting bottom—as something they thought was almost a necessity. It's as if at that moment the iron entered their soul; that moment created the resilience that leaders need.

—Warren G. Bennis

The country is full of good coaches. What it takes to win is a bunch of interested players.

—Don Coryell

Each warrior wants to leave the mark of his will, his signature, on important acts he touches. This is not the voice of ego but of the human spirit, rising up and declaring that it has something to contribute to the solution of the hardest problems, no matter how vexing!

—Pat Riley

You do not merely want to be considered just the best of the best. You want to be considered the only ones who do what you do.

—Jerry Garcia

You have to perform at a consistently higher level than others. That's the mark of a true professional.

—Joe Paterno

The place to improve the world is first in one's own heart and head and hands.

—Robert M. Pirsig

Leadership is intangible, and therefore no weapon ever designed can replace it.

—Omar Bradley

If you don't realize you can kill someone with a bokken, I don't want you using one in "MY" dojo

—Frederick J. Lovret

I will always be someone who wants to do better than others. I love competition.

—Jean-Claude Killy

Great leaders are almost always great simplifiers, who can cut through argument, debate and doubt, to offer a solution everybody can understand.

—Colin Powell

The key to successful leadership today is influence, not authority.

—Kenneth Blanchard

I am personally convinced that one person can be a change catalyst, a 'transformer' in any situation, any organization. Such an individual is yeast that can leaven an entire loaf. It requires vision, initiative, patience, respect, persistence, courage, and faith to be a transforming leader.

—Stephen R. Covey.

If you can't get them to salute when they should salute and wear the clothes you tell them to wear, how are you going to get them to die for their country?

—General George S. Patton, Jr.

The way a team plays as a whole determines its success. You may have the greatest bunch of individual stars in the world, but if they don't play together, the club won't be worth a dime.

—Babe Ruth

No man is fit to command another that cannot command himself.

—William Penn

I don't mind being called tough, since I find in this racket it's the tough guys who lead the survivors.

—Curtis LeMay

You don't have to hold a position to be a leader.

—Anthony J. D'Angelo

Explain it as we may, a martial strain will urge a man into the front rank of battle sooner than an argument, and a fine anthem excite his devotion more certainly than a logical discourse.

—Henry Tuckerman

Whatever course you have chosen for yourself, it will not be a chore but an adventure if you bring to it a sense of the glory of striving, if your sights are set far above the merely secure and mediocre.

—David Sarnoff

Be an example to your men, in your duty and in private life. Never spare yourself, and let the troops see that you don't in your endurance of fatigue and privation. always be tactful and well-mannered and teach your subordinates to do the same. Avoid excessive sharpness or harshness of voice, which usually indicates the man who has shortcomings of his own to hide.

—Field Marshall Erwin Rommel

The function of leadership is to produce more leaders, not more followers.

—Ralph Nader

We must all hang together, or assuredly we shall all hang separately

—Benjamin Franklin


If I do my full duty, the rest will take care of itself.

—George S. Patton, Jr.


On the fields of friendly strife are sown the seed that on other days and other fields will bear the fruits of victory.

—General Douglas MacArthur


There is no limit to the good you can do if you don't care who gets the credit.

—George C. Marshall


A man who has attained mastery of an art reveals it in his every action.

—Anonymous


A leader is a man who had the ability to get other people to do what they don't want to do, and like it.

—Harry S. Truman

Don't tell people how to do things, tell them what to do and let them surprise you with their results.

—George S. Patton


A leader is a dealer in hope.

—Napoleon Bonaparte


If, in order to succeed in an enterprise, I were obliged to choose between fifty deer commanded by a lion, and fifty lions commanded by a deer, I should consider myself more certain of success with the first group than with the second.

—Saint Vincent De Paul


The leader must aim high, see big, judge widely, thus setting himself apart from the ordinary people who debate in narrow confines.

—Charles De Gaulle


I must follow them. I am their leader.

—Andrew Bonar Law


Leadership is a matter of intelligence, trustworthiness, humaneness, courage, and sternness...A general should have these five virtues... Reliance on intelligence alone results in rebelliousness. Exercise of humaneness alone results in weakness. Fixation on trust results in folly. Dependence on the strength of courage results in violence. Excessive sternness in command results in cruelty. When one has all five virtues together, each appropriate to its function, then one can be a military leader.

—Sun Tzu

The number one failure of leaders is their failure to reproduce other leaders.

—Dr. Jack Elwood

Leadership, like swimming, cannot be learned by reading about it.

—Henry Mintzberg

Of the best rulers,

The people only know that they exist;

The next best they love and praise

The next they fear;

And the next they revile.

When they do not command the people's faith,

Some will lose faith in them,

And then they resort to oaths!

But of the best when their task is accomplished,

their work done,

The people all remark, "We have done it ourselves."

—Lao Tzu


The supreme quality for leadership is unquestionably integrity. Without it, no real success is possible, no matter whether it is on a section gang, a football field, in an army, or in an office.

—Dwight Eisenhower


The great leaders have always stage-managed their effects.

—Charles De Gaulle


Charisma becomes the undoing of leaders. It makes them inflexible, convinced of their own infallibility, unable to change.

—Peter F. Drucker


A leader is someone who is able to make decisions quickly, not rashly; and has enough conviction in his or her decisions that people will naturally follow a course of action. In the end, indecision and paralysis is far more costly than making an "incorrect" decision.

—John David Moore

In a moment of decision, the best thing you can do is the right thing to do. The worst thing you can do is nothing.

—Theodore Roosevelt


Leadership is not magnetic personality—that can just as well be a glib tongue. It is not 'making friends and influencing people'—that is flattery. Leadership is lifting a person's vision to higher sights, the raising of a person's performance to a higher standard, the building of a personality beyond its normal limitations.

—Peter Drucker

# 8

# *Training*

Nobody ever drowned in sweat

—U.S. Marine saying


If you train hard, you'll not only be hard, you'll be hard to beat.

—Herschel Walker


Luck is what happens when preparation meets opportunity.

—Coach Darrel Royal


Sweat plus sacrifice equals success.

—Charlie Finley


Physical fitness is not only one of the most important keys to a healthy body; it is the basis of dynamic and creative intellectual activity. The relationship between the soundness of the body and the activities of the mind is subtle and complex. Much is not yet understood. But we do know what the Greeks knew: that intelligence and skill can only function at the peak of their capacity when the body is healthy and strong; that hardy spirits and tough minds usually inhabit sound gods.

—John F. Kennedy


The will to win is important, but the will to prepare is vital.

—Joe Paterno


Perhaps the single most important element in mastering the techniques and tactics of racing is experience. But once you have the fundamentals, acquiring the experience is a matter of time.

—Greg LeMond


To be prepared is half the victory.

—Miguel Cervantes


He who stops being better stops being good.

—Oliver Cromwell


It's not necessarily the amount of time you spend at practice that counts; it's what you put into the practice.

—Eric Lindros

What we learn with pleasure we never forget.

—Louis Mercier

Practice a thousand hours and you learn self discipline.

Practice ten thousand hours and you learn about yourself.

—Myamoto Musashi

Blessed be the Lord my God,

who trains my hands to war,

and my fingers to fight

—Psalm 144:1

You may train for a long time, but if you merely move your hands and feet and jump up and down like a puppet, learning karate is not very different from learning a dance. You will never have reached the heart of the matter; you will have failed to grasp the quintessence of karate-do.

—Gichin Funakoshi

Ability without effort is a waste, yet ability combined with effort is achievement.

—Author Unknown

You are reconsidering your training, or perhaps even contemplating beginning a new system. You have been told by the teacher that to obtain proficiency, you may have to train hard for the next two to three years. You begin to wonder if all of that time out of your life is really worth it. No matter what your choice is, you're going end up there anyway in two to three years with or without the training.

—Michael R. Boyce

It should be easy to spot a black belt in a crowd; s/he should walk like a Marine on roller skates.

—Fredrick Lovret

The more I train, the more I realize I have more speed in me.

—Leroy Burrell

The best and fastest way to learn a sport is to watch and imitate a champion.

—Jean-Claude Killy

The style is not the answer. Each method has a message.

—Tony Blauer

Ultimately, you must forget about technique. The further you progress, the fewer teachings there are. The Great Path is really No Path.

—Ueshiba, Morihei

Progress comes to those who train and train. Reliance on secret techniques will get you nowhere.

—Ueshiba, Morihei

A good day is one filled with laughter and sweat.

—Dan Millman

Tomorrow's battle is won during today's practice.

—Samurai maxim

If, you can't sleep, then get up and do something instead of lying there worrying. It's the worry that gets you, not the lack of sleep.

—Dale Carnegie

Failure is the key to success; each mistake teaches us something.

—Ueshiba, Morihei

Civilize the mind but make savage the body

—Chairman Mao

The purpose of training is to tighten up the slack, toughen the body, and polish the spirit.

—Ueshiba, Morihei

Iron is full of impurities that weaken it; through forging, it becomes steel and is transformed into razor-sharp sword. Human beings develop in the same fashion.

Instructors can impart only a fraction of the teaching. It is through your own devoted practice that the mysteries of Aikido are brought to life.

—Ueshiba, Morihei

Five Secrets of Japanese Goju Ryu.

Move quickly.

Sound, calm mind.

Be light in body.

Have a clever mind.

Master the basics.

—Yamaguchi, Gogen

Even though our path is completely different from the warrior arts of the past, it is not necessary to abandon totally the old ways. Absorb venerable traditions into this Art by clothing them with fresh garments, and build on the classic styles to create better forms.

—Ueshiba, Morihei

Day after day train your heart out, refining your technique: Use the One to strike the Many! That is the discipline of the Warrior.

—Ueshiba, Morihei

The past is an illusion. You must learn to live in the present and accept yourself for what you are now. What you lack in flexibility and agility you must make up with knowledge and constant practice.

—Bruce Lee

The more you sweat in training, the less you bleed in battle.

—U.S. Navy SEAL maxim

Pain is weakness leaving your body.

—U.S. Marine Corps maxim

Life itself is always a trial. In training, you must test and polish yourself in order to face the great challenges of life. Transcend the realm of life and death, and then you will be able to make your way calmly and safely through any crisis that confronts you.

—Ueshiba, Morihei

Men give me credit for some genius. All the genius I have lies in this; when I have a subject in hand, I study it profoundly. Day and night it is before me. My mind becomes pervaded with it. Then the effort that I have made is what people are pleased to call genius.

—Alexander Hamilton

Excellence is an art won by training and habituation. We do not act rightly because we have virtue or excellence, but we rather have those because we have acted rightly. We are what we repeatedly do. Excellence, then, is not an act but a habit.

—Aristotle

You will never find time for anything. You must make it.

—Charles Buxton

# 9

## *Perseverance*

Do not let what you cannot do interfere with what you can do.

—John Wooden


The game isn't over till it's over.

—Yogi Berra


Adversity causes some men to break; others to break records.

—William A. Ward


My motto was always to keep swinging. Whether I was in a slump or feeling badly or having trouble off the field, the only thing to do was keep swinging

—Hank Aaron

When I fall on my face from time to time, I try not to worry because I'm still going forward!

—Linda Aucoin

It is a rough road that leads to the heights of greatness. ·

—Seneca

Great works are performed not by strength but by perseverance.

—Samuel Johnson

The only way to overcome is to hang in. Even I'm starting to believe that.

—Dan O'Brien

Nothing in the world can take the place of persistence. Talent will not: Nothing is more common than unsuccessful men with talent. Genius will not: Un-rewarded genius is almost a proverb. Education will not: The world is full of educated derelicts. Persistence and determination alone are omnipotent.

—Calvin Coolidge

If at first you don't succeed, you are running about average.

—M.H. Alderson

I think and think for months and years. Ninety-nine times the conclusion is false. The hundredth time I am right.

—Albert Einstein

Of those who start TaeKwonDo training, only about 5% stick with it until they achieve the Black Belt Rank. Then perhaps 80% of those who earn a Black stop there.

—Duk Sung Son

1-2 out of every 100 students reach Black Belt and of those only 1 out of every 1,000 achieves his 2nd Dan.

—Masutatsu Oyama

Success seems to be largely a matter of hanging on after others have let go.

—William Feather

Fire is the test of gold, adversity, of strong men.

—Seneca

The difference between the impossible and the possible lies in a man's determination

—Tommy Lasorda

I've always made a total effort, even when the odds seemed entirely against me. I never quit trying; I never felt that I didn't have a chance to win.

—Arnold Palmer

It's hard to beat a person who never gives up.

—Babe Ruth

So long as there is breath in me, that long will I persist. For now I know one of the greatest principles of success; If I persist long enough I will win.

—Og Mandino

Genius is one percent inspiration and ninety-nine percent perspiration.

—Thomas Edison

You get credit for what you finish, not what you start.

—Anonymous

Move—one step at a time, but always forward.

—Anonymous

It's a little like wrestling a gorilla. You don't quit when you're tired—you quit when the gorilla is tired.

—Robert Strauss

No matter how long the river, the river will reach the sea.

—Eugene Fitch Ware

Winners never quit and quitters never win.

—Unknown

Never discourage anyone who continually makes progress, no matter how slow.

—Plato

The difference between a successful person and others is not a lack of strength, not a lack of knowledge, but rather a lack of will.

—Vincent T. Lombardi

Defeat is a state of mind. No one is ever defeated until defeat has been accepted as a reality. To me, defeat in anything is merely temporary, and its punishment is but an urge for me to greater effort to achieve my goal. Defeat simply tells me that something is wrong in my doing; it is a path leading to success and truth.

—Bruce Lee


Other people may not have had high expectations for me…but I had high expectations for myself.

—Shannon Miller


In order to win you must be prepared to lose sometime. And leave one or two cards showing.

—Van Morrison


You may have to fight a battle more than once to win it.

—Margaret Thatcher


I have learned that success is to be measured not so much by the position that one has reached in life as by the obstacles which he has overcome while trying to succeed.

—Booker T. Washington

Never, never, never give up.

—Winston Churchill

Develop an attitude of gratitude, and give thanks for everything that happens to you, knowing that every step forward is a step toward achieving something bigger and better than your current situation.

—Brian Tracy

Lord, grant that I may always desire more than I accomplish.

—Michelangelo

Bad times have a value. These are occasions a good learner would not miss.

—Ralph Waldo Emerson

If you hear a voice within you say 'you cannot paint,' then by all means paint, and that voice will be silenced.

—Vincent Van Gogh

# 10

## *Mind*

One mind, any weapon

—Hunter B. Armstrong

You are searching for the magic key that will unlock the door to the source of power; and yet you have the key in your own hands, and you may use it the moment you learn to control your thoughts.

—Napoleon Hill

No great improvements in the lot of mankind are possible until a great change takes place in the fundamental constitution of their modes of thought.

—John Stuart Mill

Any fact not facing us is not as important as our attitude toward it, for that determines our success or failure.

—Norman Vincent Peale

The mind is the limit. As long as the mind can envision the fact that you can do something, you can do it—as long as you really believe 100 percent.

—Arnold Schwarzenegger

Empty your mind, be formless, shapeless like water. Now you put water into a cup, it becomes the cup. You put water into a bottle, it becomes the bottle. You put it in a teapot, it becomes the teapot. Now water can flow, or it can crash! Be water, my friend.

—Bruce Lee

I'm moving and not moving at all. I'm like the moon underneath the waves that ever go on rolling and rocking. It is not, "I am doing this," but rather, an inner realization that "this is happening through me," or "it is doing this for me." The consciousness of self is the greatest hindrance to the proper execution of all physical action.

—Bruce Lee

Concentration is the ability to think about absolutely nothing when it is absolutely necessary.

—Ray Knight

If you can believe it, the mind can achieve it.

—Ronnie Lott

If you think you can win, you can win. Faith is necessary to victory.

—William Hazlitt

A mind troubled by doubt cannot focus on the course to victory

—Arthur Golden

All men dream: But not equally. Those who dream by night in the dusty recess of their minds wake in the day to find it was vanity: But the dreamers of the day are dangerous men for they may act their dreams with open eyes, to make it possible.

—Thomas Lawrence

The winners in life think constantly in terms of I can, I will, and I am. Losers, on the other hand, concentrate their waking thoughts on what they should have or would have done, or what they can't do.

—Dennis Waitley

Believe Big. The size of your success is determined by the size of your belief. Think little goals and expect little achievements. Think big goals and win big success. Remember this, too! Big ideas and bigplans are often easier—certainly no more difficult—than small ideas and small plans.

—David Schwartz

A black belt is nothing more than a belt that goes around your waist. Being a black belt is a state of mind and attitude.

—Rick English

In Judo, he who thinks is immediately thrown.

—Robert Linssen

The sword has to be more than a simple weapon; it has to be an answer to life's questions.

—Musashi, Miyamoto

The way of the sword and the Way of Zen are identical, for they have the same purpose; that of killing the ego.

—Yamada, Jirokichi

Every man today is the results of his thoughts from yesterday.

—Anonymous

The art of the sword consists of never being concerned with victory or defeat, with strength or weakness, of not moving one step forward, nor one step backward, or the enemy not seeing me and my not seeing the enemy. Penetrating to that which is fundamental before the separation of heaven and earth where even yin and yang cannot reach, one instantly attains proficiency in the art.

—Takuan

You have to expect things of yourself before you can do them.

—Michael Jordan

Give up thinking as though not giving it up. Observe techniques as though not observing.

—Bruce Lee

Eliminate "not clear" thinking and function from your root.

—Bruce Lee

I always felt that my greatest asset was not my physical ability, it was my mental ability.

—Bruce Jenner

A child's attitude toward everything is an artist's attitude.

—Willa Cather

In the beginner's mind there are many possibilities, but in the expert's there are few.

—Suzuki, Shunryu

In a fight between a strong technique and a strong body, technique will prevail. In a fight between a strong mind and a strong technique, mind will prevail, because it will find the weak point.

—Taisen Deshimaru

I think I've always had the shots. But in the past, I've suffered too many mental lapses. Now, I'm starting to get away from that and my mental discipline and commitment to the game are much better. I think I'm really taking a good look at the big picture. That's the difference between being around for the final or watching the final from my sofa at home.

—Andre Agassi

Think big, believe big, act big, and the results will be big.

—Anonymous

Winning isn't everything, wanting to is.

—Anonymous

If you walk, just walk. If you sit, just sit. But whatever you do, don't wobble.

—Master Ummon


A good stance and posture reflect a proper state of mind.

—Ueshiba, Morihei


He who fumes at his quandaries becomes their victim.

—David Seabury


He Who Knows Others Is Wise. He Who Knows Himself Is Enlightened.

—Tao Te Ching


Truth has no path. Truth is living and, therefore, changing. Awareness is without choice, without demand, without anxiety; in that state of mind, there is perception. To know oneself is to study oneself in action with another person. Awareness has no frontier; it is giving of your whole being, without exclusion.

—Bruce Lee

Fear is the mind killer.

—Frank Herbert


The greatest mistake you can make in this life is to be continually fearing you will make one.

—Elbert Hubbard


Learn to control your emotions or they will control you.

—Edgar Martinez.


It's a difficult thing to truly know your own limits and points of weakness.

—Hagakure


The most important part of a player's body is above his shoulders.

—Ty Cobb


Mentally I try to stay at a medium level, not too high or too low.

—Todd Zeile

You have to expect things of yourself before you can do them.

—Michael Jordan


When attacking, don't be careless.

—The Way of the Spear


Turn into a doll made of wood: it has no ego, it thinks nothing, it is not grasping or sticky. Let the body and limbs work theselves out in accordance with the discipline they have undergone.

—Bruce Lee


Act like a man of thought—Think like a man of action

—Thomas Mann


Why do some people always see beautiful skies and grass and lovely flowers and incredible human beings, while others are hard-pressed to find anything or any place that is beautiful?

—Leo Buscaglia

When two opponents of equal stregnth and technique fight it off: it is what is in their heart, and how they use their mind, that will decide who will win.

—Bruce Hyland

Conversation was never begun at once, nor in a hurried manner. No one was quick with a question, no matter how important, and no one was pressed for an answer. A pause giving time for thought was the truly courteous way of beginning and conducting a conversation. Silence was meaningful with the Lakota, and his granting a space of silence to the speech-maker and his own moment of silence before talking was done in the practice of true politeness and regard for the rule that "thought comes before speech."

—Luther Standing Bear

Everything—mountains, rivers, plants, trees—should be your teacher.

—Ueshiba, Morihei

The biggest thing is to have a mind-set and a belief you can win any tournament going in.

—Tiger Woods

I don't think of all the misery but of the beauty that still remains.

—Anne Frank

What you are thinking, what shape your mind is in, is what makes the biggest difference of all.

—Willie Mays

When you follow your bliss, doors will open where you would not have thought there would be doors; and where there wouldn't be a door for anyone else.

—Joseph Campbell

# 11

## *Humor*

It is not the fall that kills you. It is the realization that "yes, you did something that stupid."

—Anonymous

There are two rules for being successful in Martial Arts.

Rule 1: Never tell others everything you know.

—Anonymous

We staunch traditionalists know that appearance is everything. Technique is nowhere near as important as having your pleats straight when you die

—Steve Gombosi

If you can't beat your computer at chess, try kick-boxing

—Anonymous

The race may not always be to the swift nor the victory to the strong, but that's how you bet.

—Damon Runyon

"Ow" is not a Kempo word

—Jonathan Vance

That which does not kill us, must have missed us.

—Miowara Tomokata

A language is a dialect that has an army and navy.

—Max Weinreich

It's just a job. Grass grows, birds fly, waves pound the sand. I beat people up.

—Muhammad Ali

The world is full of willing people, some willing to work, the others willing to let them.

—Robert Frost

Nobody climbs mountains for scientific reasons. Science is used to raise money for the expeditions, but you really climb for the hell of it.

—Sir Edmund Hillary

Even if you are on the right track, you'll get run over if you just sit there.

—Will Rogers

Always forgive your enemies—Nothing annoys them so much.

—Oscar Wilde

I believe in getting into hot water. I think it keeps you clean.

—G. K. Chesterton

Karate is a form of martial arts in which people who have had years and years of training can, using only their hands and feet, make some of the worst movies in the history of the world.

—Dave Barry

The power of accurate observation is commonly called cynicism by those who have not got it.

—George Bernard Shaw

Good…Bad…I'm the guy with the gun.

—Ash, from Army of Darkness

The trouble with political jokes is that very often they get elected.

—Will Rogers

You need to defend these people…It could be that the attacker is trying to get through me to these other people, who aren't trained to fight, but they're good people, so I have to protect them. Or maybe they're not good people, they're cannibals…but they're my friends.

—Ken Doyle

This man is a human being. He may have friends, a loving family, and deep down he's probably a decent person, one day he might even find the cure for cancer. But we don't know…and WE DON'T CARE. He has made a choice…the wrong one…AND NOW HE MUST DIE.

—Ken Doyle

You might be a martial artist if….

1) You find yourself casually standing in a half cat stance.

2) You trip, go into a roll and come up in a fighting stance. In church.

3) You answer your boss Ussss.

4) You put your hands together in a martial arts bow position (one hand open the other closed) after grace at the dinner table.

5) You tie your bathrobe belt in a square knot. Then check to make sure the ends are exactly even.

6) You accept change from the cashier using a perfect knife hand with the thumb carefully tucked in.

7) Every time you handle a screwdriver or razor knife, etc. You just can't help changing grip from hammer to reverse to flip over to dagger grip etc. And your shop help is standing cautiously far, far away from you.

8) When you're outside doing landscaping/gardening you "practice" with all the neat weapons

—Anonymous


Here are some sign that you have been on the martial arts path a little too long:

1) When you are being thrown, you shout, "Wahoo!"

2) You laugh when you are hit in the head.

3) When leaving your orthopedist's office after your final treatment, she says, "See you next time."

4) You try to teach your pet to bow to you.

5) You look at everyone as a potential attacker, especially the grand-mothers (You know, expect the unexpected).

—Anonymous

I went to a fight the other night and a hockey game broke out.

—Rodney Dangerfield

If at first you don't succeed...So much for skydiving.

—Henry Youngman

Jerry: (to Kramer) So how's your karate class going?

Kramer: (pronouncing it "kar-ah-tay") Karate, Jerry. Karate. The life-time pursuit of balance and harmony.

Jerry: ...But with punching and kicking.

—Seinfeld

Murphy's Laws of Martial Arts

Ten scientific principles that apply to the study of all martial arts:

1. The wimp who made it through the eliminations on luck alone will suddenly turn into Bruce Lee when you're up against him.

2. The referee will always be looking the other way when you score.

3. You will have trouble with the ties on your gi pants when members of the opposite sex are in class.

4. The day you leave work early to make it to class on time, the sensei will be sick.

5.  The sensei will only use you during demonstrations for joint-locking techniques.

6.  If you have to use your training in self-defense, your attacker's father will be a lawyer.

7.  After a flawless demonstration, you will trip on your way back to your seat.

8.  After years of training without a single injury, you will pull a groin muscle the night before your black belt exam.

9.  In an otherwise vacant locker room, the only other person will have the locker right next to yours.

10. No matter how many times you take care of it before your promotion exam, you will invariably have to go to the bathroom when it's your turn.

—Anonymous


You can get more with a kind word and a gun than you can with a kind word alone.

—Al Capone


Deja Fu: The feeling that somehow, somewhere, you've been kicked in the head like this before.

—Anonymous

# 12

## *Wisdom*

It is not the accumulation of extraneous knowledge, but the realization of the self within, that constitutes true progress.

—Okakura Kakuzo

A man of knowledge chooses a path with a heart and follows it and then he looks and rejoices and laughs and then he sees and knows.

He knows that his life will be over altogether too soon.

He knows that he as well as everybody else is not going anywhere.

He knows because he sees.

A man of knowledge endeavors and sweats and puffs and if one looks at him he is just like any ordinary man, except that the folly of his life is under control.

—don Juan via Carlos Castenada

It's what you learn after you know everything that counts.

—John Wooden

When people are fanatically dedicated to political or religious faiths or any other kinds of dogmas or goals, it's always because these dogmas or goals are in doubt.

—Robert Pirsig


To be what we are, and to become what we are capable of becoming, is the only end of life.

—Robert Louis Stevenson


The opposite of a correct statement is a false statement. The opposite of a profound truth may well be another profound truth.

—Niels Bohr


To understand others is to be knowledgeable;

To understand yourself is to be wise;

To conquer others is to have strength;

To conquer yourself is to be strong

—Lao Tzu

If you can show me a person who has made no mistakes,

I will show you a person who has achieved nothing.

—Anonymous


Traditionalists often study what is taught, not what there is to create.

—Ed Parker


Now and again, it is necessary to seclude yourself among deep mountains and hidden valleys to restore your link to the source of life.

—Ueshiba, Morihei


No one nation or people has a monopoly on the sun and no one art or system as a monopoly on truth.

—Mike Casto


Truth is universal. Perception of truth is not.

—Anonymous

Your opinion is your opinion, your perception is your perception—do not confuse them with "facts" or "truth". Wars have been fought and millions have been killed because of the inability of men to understand the idea that EVERYBODY has a different viewpoint.

—John Moore

You are enrolled in a full-time informal school called LIFE. Each day in this school, you will have the opportunity to learn lessons. You may like the lessons or think them irrelevant and stupid

—Seneca Wolf Clan Teaching Lodge

Tolerance is the positive and cordial effort to understand another's beliefs, practices and habits without necessarily sharing or accepting them.

—Joshua Loth Liebman

Live as if you were to die tomorrow.

Learn as if you were to live forever.

—Mahatma Gandhi

Without Knowledge, Skill cannot be focused. Without Skill, Strength cannot be brought to bear and without Strength, Knowledge may not be applied.

—Alexander the Great's Chief Physician

Nature has given us two ears, two eyes, and but one tongue, to the end that we should hear and see more than we speak.

—Socrates

We are much better than we know.

—Lance Armstrong

Trouble no more about their religion; respect others in their view, and demand that they respect yours.

—Tecumseh

Man has responsibility, not power.

—Native American Proverb

My life is simple, my food is plain, and my quarters are uncluttered. In all things, I have sought clarity. I face the troubles and problems of life and death willingly. Virtue, integrity and courage are my priorities. I can be approached, but never pushed; befriended but never coerced; killed but never shamed.

—Yi Sunshin

When you have fun, it changes all the pressure into pleasure.

—Ken Griffey Sr. and Ken Griffey Jr.

Humankind has not woven the web of life. We are but one thread within it. Whatever we do to the web, we do to ourselves. All things are bound together. All things connect.

—Seattle

Given enough time, any man may master the physical. With enough knowledge, any man may become wise. It is the true warrior who can master both…and surpass the result.

—Tien T'ai

It is difficult to say what is impossible, for the dream of yesterday is the hope of today and the reality of tomorrow.

—Robert Goddard

He is truly wise who gains wisdom from another's mishap.

—Publilius Cyrus

For want of a nail, the shoe was lost; For want of a shoe, the horse was lost; For want of a horse, the rider was lost; For want of a rider, the battle was lost.

—Benjamin Franklin

If nothing within you stays rigid, outward things will disclose themselves. Moving, be like water. Still, be like a mirror. Respond like an echo.

—Bruce Lee

The man who can't make a mistake can't make anything.

—Abraham Lincoln

A one sided martial artist is a blind martial artist.

—Anonymous

If you know the art of breathing you have the strength, wisdom and courage of ten tigers.

—Chinese adage

I am a Shawnee. My forefathers were warriors. Their son is a warrior. From my tribe I take nothing. I am the maker of my own fortune.

—Tecumseh

There is no death. Only a change of worlds.

—Seattle

To win one hundred victories in one hundred battles is not the highest skill. To subdue the enemy without fighting is the highest skill.

—Sun-Tsu

To change with change is the changeless state.

—Anonymous

The Way of a Warrior cannot be encompassed by words or in letters: grasp the essence and move on toward realization!

—Ueshiba, Morihei

The fact that you are willing to say, "I do not understand, and it is fine," is the greatest understanding you could exhibit.

—Wayne Dyer

Please do not be concerned with soft versus firm, kicking versus striking, grappling versus hitting and kicking, long-range fighting versus infighting. There is no such thing as "this" is better than "that". Should there be one thing we must guard against, let it be partiality that robs us of our pristine wholeness and make us lose unity in the midst of duality.

—Bruce Lee


Budo is supposed to enhance your life, not replace it.

—F. J. Lovret


If we are once successful at something we naturally will repeat that action despite its inefficiency.

—Ken Doyle


A prudent question is one-half of wisdom.

—Francis Bacon


He that cannot reason is a fool. He that will not is a bigot. He that dare not is a slave.

—Andrew Carnegie

In the practice of tolerance, one's enemy is the best teacher.

—H.H. the Dalai Lama

The man that conquers himself is superior to the one who conquers a thousand men in battle.

—Buddha

The Way of the warrior does not include other ways, such as Confucianism, Buddhism, certain traditions, artistic accomplishments, and dancing. But even though these are not part of the Way, if you know the Way broadly, you will see it in everything.

—Musashi, Miyamoto

If you won't be better tomorrow than you were today, then what do you need tomorrow for?

—Rebbe Nachman of Breslov

Finish each day and be done with it. You have done what you could; some blunders and absurdities have crept in; forget them as soon as you can. Tomorrow is a new day; you shall begin it serenely and with too high a spirit to be encumbered with your old nonsense.

—Ralph Waldo Emerson

The truth of the matter is that you always know the right thing to do.
The hard part is doing it.

—H. Norman Schwarzkopf

# 13

## *Peace*

Get rid of "altruism" and abandon "Justice" and the people will return to filial piety and compassion.

—Lao Tzu, Tao te ching

The Art of Peace is medicine for a sick world. There is evil and disorder in the world, because people have forgotten that all things emanate from one source. Return to that source and leave behind all self-centered thoughts, petty desires, and anger. Those who are possessed by nothing possess everything.

—Ueshiba, Morihei

Patriotism is not enough. I must have no hatred or bitterness towards anyone.

—Edith Cavell

War is hell.

—William Tecumseh Sherman

To be prepared for war is one of the most effectual means of preserving peace.

—General George Washington

Victory attained by violence is tantamount to a defeat, for it is momentary.

—Mahatma Ghandi

Arms are instruments of ill omen.... When one is compelled to use them, it is best to do so without relish. There is no glory in victory, and to glorify it despite this is to exult in the killing of men.... When great numbers of people are killed, one should weep over them with sorrow. When victorious in war, one should observe mourning rites.

—Lao Tsu

Ahisma, "non-violence," is therefore much more than the absence of destruction. It is the absence of the desire to destroy.

—Mark Juergensmeyer

The fastest draw is when the sword never leaves the scabbard, the strongest way to block, is never to provoke a blow, and the cleanest cut is the one withheld.

—Anonymous

Budo is not a means of felling the opponent by force or by lethal weapons. Neither is it intended to lead the world to destruction by arms and other illegitimate means. True Budo calls for bringing the inner energy of the universe in order, protecting the peace of the world and molding, as well as preserving, everything in nature in its right form.

—Ueshiba, Morihei

If one is without kindness, how can one be called a human being?

—Sarada Devi

Am I not destroying my enemies when I make friends of them?

—Abraham Lincoln

The fire of anger only burns the angry.

—Chinese Proverb

War is the child of pride.

—Anonymous

The war has already almost destroyed that nation…I have seen, I guess, as much blood and disaster as any living man, and it just turned my stomach the last time I was there. After I looked at that wreckage and those thousands of women and children and everything, I vomited.

—Douglas MacArthur


Discourage litigation. Persuade your neighbors to compromise whenever you can. As a peacemaker the lawyer has superior opportunity of being a good man. There will still be business enough.

—Abraham Lincoln

# *About the Author*

John David Moore is a personal protection instructor and co-founder of Martial Training Systems LLC. He is a recognized expert in self-defense who has conducted training seminars throughout New England. His particular focus is on violence prevention through awareness training and performance psychology.

Mr. Moore is a member of the American Jujutsu Association, The American Psychological Association, and the American Society for Law Enforcement Training. He has trained in martial arts since the age of 10, studying under world-class instructors such as Sensei Peter Freedman, Guro George Brewster, and Tony Blauer. He also is a nationally certified fitness instructor.

In addition to this, Mr. Moore is set to complete a Masters Degree in dispute resolution in 2003. He is currently working on a thesis project involving the prevention of workplace violence. In 2002, Mr. Moore presented a paper at a conflict resolution conference on the link between Internet behavior and real-world violence.

Mr. Moore, along with his partners at Martial Training Systems are currently in development of several new personal protection and physical conditioning training systems. Due to be released in early 2003, please see their web site at **www.martialtrainingsystems.com**.

0-595-26492-1

Printed in the United States
972700004B